ARGENTINA
the land

Greg Nickles

A Bobbie Kalman Book

The Lands, Peoples, and Cultures Series

 Crabtree Publishing Company

www.crabtreebooks.com

The Lands, Peoples, and Cultures Series

Created by Bobbie Kalman

Coordinating editor
Ellen Rodger

Project development, photo research, and design
First Folio Resource Group, Inc.
  Erinn Banting
  Pauline Beggs
  Tom Dart
  Kathryn Lane
  Alana Perez
  Debbie Smith

Editing
Jessica Rudolph

Separations and film
Embassy Graphics

Printer
Worzalla Publishing Company

Consultants
Pampa Risso Patrón, Pan American Cultural Exchange, Houston, Texas; Roberto Risso Patrón; Diana Pelenur, Consulate General of the Republic of Argentina in Montreal

Photographs
AP/Wide World Photo: p. 11 (left); Corbis/Neil Beer: cover; Corbis/Pablo Corral V: p. 15 (bottom); Corbis/Yann Arthus-Bertrand: p. 17 (bottom); Corbis/Enzo & Paolo Ragazzini: p. 4, p. 19; Corbis/Hubert Stadler: p. 17 (top), p. 23 (top); Corbis/Robert van der Hilst: p. 3; Tim Davis/Photo Researchers: p. 9; Fletcher & Baylis, The National Audubon Society Collection/Photo Researchers: p. 29 (left); Robert Fried/DDB Stock Photo: p. 14; Pablo Garber: p. 21 (bottom), p. 23 (top left), p. 26 (bottom); Carlos Goldin/DDB Stock Photo: p. 12 (right), p. 27 (top); François Gohier, The National Audubon Society Collection/Photo Researchers: p. 29 (right); Mark Harvey: p. 5 (middle), p. 7 (bottom); George Holton, The National Audubon Society Collection/Photo Researchers: p. 31 (top left); Max & Bea Hunn/DDB Stock Photo: p. 16 (top); Hugo Lazaridis/LZ Producciones: p. 13 (bottom), p. 15 (top); Michael Moody/DDB Stock Photo: p. 16 (bottom); Julio Pantoja/Infoto: p. 10 (right), p. 12 (left), p. 20 (bottom), p. 21 (top), p. 23 (bottom), p. 26 (top); Daniel Rivademar/Odyssey Productions: title page, p. 24 (top), p. 28; Daniel Rodriguez/LZ Producciones: p. 18; Jasmine Rossi: p. 5 (top, bottom), p. 7 (top), p. 8 (both), p. 30 (both); Chris R. Sharp/DDB Stock Photo: p. 20 (top); The Secretariat of Tourism of Argentina: p. 13 (top), p. 31 (bottom left); Nestor Troncoso/LZ Producciones: p. 24 (bottom); Art Wolfe, The National Audubon Society/Photo Researchers: p. 31 (right); Leonardo Zavattaro/LZ Producciones: p. 10 (left), p. 11 (right), p. 22, p. 25, p. 27 (bottom)

Map
Jim Chernishenko

Illustrations
Dianne Eastman: icon
David Wysotski, Allure Illustrations: back cover

Cover: Large chunks of ice fall from the Perito Mareno glacier, in southern Argentina, into the waters below.

Title page: The Río Negro rushes through the Río Azul valley in central Argentina.

Icon: An ombu, which is a giant herb, appears at the head of each section.

Back cover: The nine-banded armadillo is protected by an armor made up of nine individual plates, or sections.

Published by
Crabtree Publishing Company

PMB 16A
350 Fifth Avenue
Suite 3308
New York
N.Y. 10118

612 Welland Avenue
St. Catharines
Ontario, Canada
L2M 5V6

73 Lime Walk
Headington
Oxford OX3 7AD
United Kingdom

Cataloging in Publication Data
Nickles, Greg, 1969-
    Argentina: the land/Greg Nickles.
    p.cm. -- (The lands, peoples, and cultures series)
Includes index.
    ISBN 0-86505-244-1 (RLB) -- ISBN 0-86505-324-3 (pbk.)
    1. Argentina--Description and travel--Juvenile literature. [1
Argentina. I. Title. II. Series.
F2808.2 .N53 2000
982--dc21

00-D43221
LC

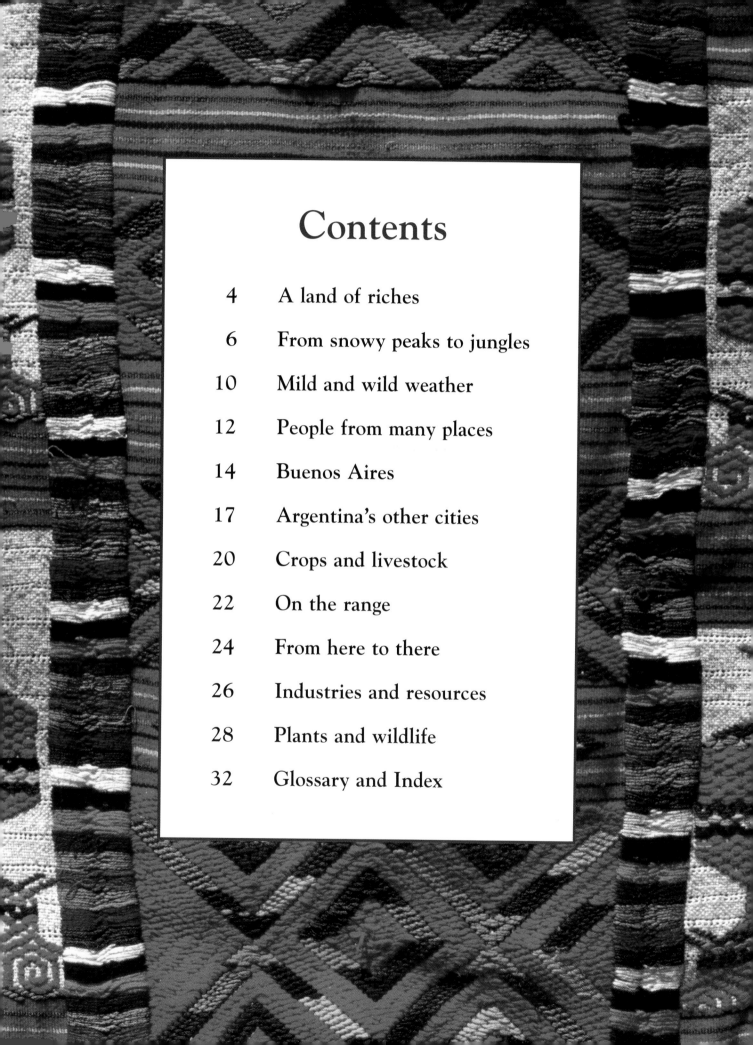

Contents

A land of riches

Argentina has an amazing variety of landscapes. From evergreen rain forests in the **tropical** north, the land stretches south to stormy Cape Horn, near the icy continent of Antarctica. Rugged mountains tower in the west, while sunny beaches and sheer cliffs stretch along the east coast. Vast plains roll gently across the middle of the country and deserts spread through the south. In addition to its natural splendor, Argentina has one of the largest and most exciting cities in the world — its **capital**, Buenos Aires.

The Silver Land

Argentina's name comes from *argentum*, a Latin word that means "silver." Spanish explorers first used the name when they arrived in the 1500s in search of riches. They found no silver, but continued to use the name "Argentina" to describe the region. In time, people realized that Argentina's greatest resource was not its silver, but its other **minerals** and **fertile** land.

Facts at a glance

Official name: *Republica Argentina* (Argentine Republic)
Area: 1,068,300 square miles (2,766,890 square kilometers)
Population: 36,737,664
Capital city: Buenos Aires
Official language: Spanish
Main religion: Roman Catholicism
Currency: peso argentino (Argentine peso)
National holidays: May 25 (Revolution Day), June 20 (Flag Day), and July 9 (Independence Day)

Red cliffs stand along the river of Conchas near Salta, in northern Argentina.

4

(above) Unusual rock formations are scattered throughout the rugged valleys of the Andes mountains.

(right) Trees line the Río Blanco, which flows through the mountainous region of Neuquén, in southern Argentina.

(below) Sheer cliffs rise along Patagonia's coastline.

From snowy peaks to jungles

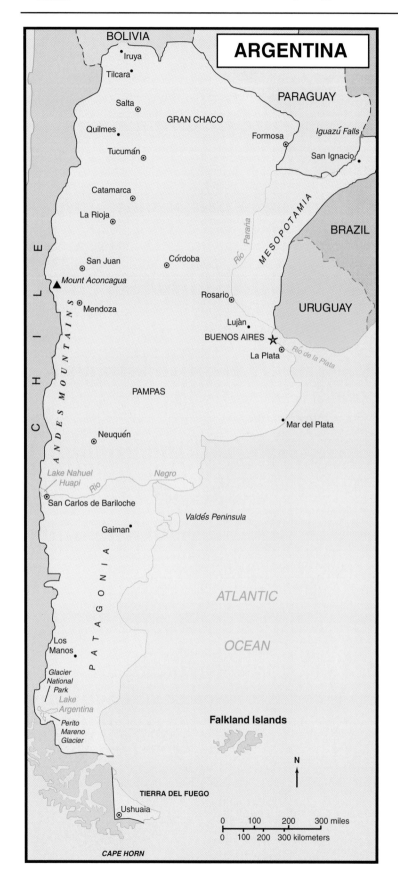

Argentina is made up of several geographical areas, each with its own landforms and plant life. From north to south, the main regions are the lowlands of the Gran Chaco and Mesopotamia, the vast Pampa plains, the Andes mountains, remote Patagonia, and the island of Tierra del Fuego.

The Gran Chaco

Most of the hot Gran Chaco region, in the north, is a lowland area covered by grass and large scrub forests where low trees and shrubs grow. Gorges, cliffs, and rivers, some surrounded by swampland, break up the landscape. Ancient seas once flowed here, but all that remain are large, flat areas covered with layers of salt. High above the lowlands stands the world's tallest volcano, the 22,869-foot (6,930-meter) Ojos del Salado.

Mesopotamia

Mesopotamia, in the northeast, is a hot, wet region filled with jungles, swamps, and grasslands. It is named after a region in southwest Asia, which, like the Argentine Mesopotamia, lies between two rivers and is extremely fertile. Tropical trees and flowers, as well as oranges, lemons, rice, and tea, thrive in Mesopotamia's humidity and rich, red soil.

Along Mesopotamia's northern border, amidst jungles filled with monkeys, wildcats, and colorful birds, roars one of the world's most spectacular waterfalls. The Iguazú Falls is made up of 275 individual waterfalls, which cover an area twice as wide as North America's Niagara Falls.

The Pampa plains

In the center of Argentina lie the enormous, grassy Pampa plains. Only an occasional hill, tree, or windmill breaks up this flat landscape. In the western part of the plains, the land is drier and scattered with sand dunes. The country's longest river, the Paraná, runs through the Chaco, Mesopotamia, and Pampas. It joins the Uruguay River to form the Río de la Plata, which flows past Buenos Aires on its way to the Atlanic Ocean.

About two-thirds of Argentines live on the Pampa plains, mostly in Buenos Aires and other cities. The majority of Argentina's industries are based in this area, as are most of the country's farms.

In some places, the Iguazú Falls plunge more than 197 feet (60 meters).

Clumps of grasses grow tall on the fertile Pampa plains.

The Andes mountains

The breathtaking Andes mountains stretch along Argentina's entire western border. They form the longest mountain chain in the world and are the world's second-highest mountain range. Most of this beautiful region is cool and rugged. In the desertlike north, very little grows other than a few hearty plants, such as thorn bushes and cacti. In the central Andes, farmers plant fruit trees and raise **livestock**, and miners extract minerals. In the southern Andes, deep valleys shelter cold, clear lakes and enormous **glaciers**. Only a few small farms and villages are scattered throughout these giant mountains where sheep are raised.

Wild Patagonia

Patagonia lies in the isolated south of Argentina. Most of the dry, rocky landscape is covered by low bushes and coarse grasses. There are few villages, and crops grow only in the deep, sheltered **canyons** that crisscross the land.

According to legend, Patagonia got its name from the European explorer Ferdinand Magellan and his crew. When they landed on the coast of Argentina in 1520, they met members of the local Tehuelche people. After seeing the huge boots the Tehuelche wore to stay warm, the crew called the region "Patagonia," or "Land of the Big Feet."

The Andes loom high above the grassy plains of Mendoza.

Grasses and scrub bushes grow on the rocky shorelines of Patagonia.

Cargo waits to be transported from Ushuaia's port.

The Land of Fire

Off the southern tip of Argentina lies the island of Tierra del Fuego. Argentina owns the island's eastern side, and the country of Chile owns the western side. Tierra del Fuego is very wet and rugged. Cold, clear rivers flow down from its snowy mountain peaks, and dense forests cover the slopes. Fierce winter storms blow around Cape Horn, at the island's southern tip. In the midst of this forbidding climate sits Ushuaia, the world's most southerly city.

The name Tierra del Fuego, which is Spanish for "Land of Fire," was given to the island by Spanish explorers. It referred to the campfires of the local Ona and Yagane peoples, which the explorers saw burning in the hills at night.

Disputed lands

For many years, Argentina has argued with England over the ownership of the Falkland Islands in the southern Atlantic Ocean. Argentina calls these islands the Islas Malvinas. Argentina claims that the British navy forced the Argentine population out of the islands in 1833 and allowed British people to settle there. This longstanding conflict erupted into a short war in 1982. Argentina's military government tried to take possession of the islands, but Britain sent forces to protect their rule and won the Falklands back.

Mild and wild weather

Argentina's climate is different in the north, middle, and south of the country. In the north, the weather is tropical. Temperatures can reach 120° Fahrenheit (48° Celsius). In the middle of the country, temperatures are moderate. It is never too hot or too cold. The south is the coldest region. Temperatures there can drop to 3° Fahrenheit (–16° Celsius).

The climate also varies according to the altitude, or height of the land. Temperatures are colder at higher altitudes. In the Andes Mountains, for example, snow stays on the mountain peaks even during the summer.

The hot, dry zonda *winds, or* viento norte, *sweep across the Pampa plains.*

Flood!

Northeast Argentina floods from time to time. Rivers in Mesopotamia and the Gran Chaco overflow with rainwater during the summer, causing muddy water to rush through the regions.

When the wind blows

The climate in Argentina is strongly influenced by winds. Moisture-rich winds from the Atlantic Ocean, to the east, bring rain and humidity. Pacific winds cross the Andes from the west, bringing dry weather. When air from Antarctica sweeps across the country, the temperature turns cold.

People watch out for the *pampero* and *zonda* winds. The cool, stormy *pampero* rushes across the northeastern Pampa plains, bringing sheets of rain, crashing thunder, and lightning. The very warm and dry *zonda* blows through the northwest in wintertime. Although it brings clear weather, many Argentines complain that the *zonda* causes headaches and sickness.

People push their cars through waist-deep water on a flooded highway near Formosa.

Colorful umbrellas shield crowds of sunbathers on a beach in Mar del Plata, on the east coast.

The shadow

Argentina's mountain slopes are dry year-round. They sit in an area called the Andes **rain shadow**, where rain rarely falls. Winds from the Pacific Ocean dump heavy rains on the Chilean slopes of the Andes, to the west. By the time these winds cross the mountain peaks into Argentina, they have lost most of their moisture. Similarly, winds that blow from the Atlantic drop most of their moisture on the land before reaching the Andes. What little wetness this area receives comes from mountain rivers and streams, which carry meltwater down from the Andes' snowcapped peaks.

Argentina's seasons

Argentina is in the Southern Hemisphere, the half of the world that is south of the equator. Its seasons are the reverse of the seasons in North America, which lies in the Northern Hemisphere. Between December and March, while it is winter in the United States and Canada, Argentina has summer. Argentina's winter lasts from June through September.

Children in Ushuaia gather snow for a snow fort in the middle of July.

Snow and ice

The Pampa plains and the lands to the north occasionally have frost or snow, but heavy snowfalls are most common in Patagonia and in the Andes mountains. In the southern Andes, large glaciers are lodged in deep valleys. These thick, slow-moving ice sheets formed over thousands of years as new layers of snow collected and were gradually packed down to form ice. Forty-seven glaciers sit in Glacier National Park. Perito Moreno, one of the most famous glaciers, is nearly 2 miles (3 kilometers) wide and 165 feet (50 meters) thick. It creeps down the slopes of a mountain and covers part of Lake Argentino. Every few years, large ice chunks break off Perito Moreno into the lake with a thunderous crack.

People from many places

The **ancestors** of the Argentines came from many places. Some were Native peoples whose **cultures** existed in South America for thousands of years. In the 1500s, the land became part of Spain's kingdom and thousands of Spanish settlers began to arrive. The region broke away from Spain in 1816, and by the mid-1800s its government began welcoming several million **immigrants** from all over Europe. Since the mid-1900s, people have moved to Argentina from other South American countries, the Middle East, and Asia. More recently, many have come from the United States and Europe to open new businesses.

From Spain

Spanish culture has had the greatest influence on Argentina's people. Spanish settlers brought with them their language and traditions. They took over much of the countryside and built many new settlements. They also set up schools, businesses, and churches.

(right) Three friends take a break from a soccer game.

(below) Women gather beneath a tree to watch the events at a family get-together.

Some Argentines can trace their ancestry back to Spanish settlers who came to South America almost 500 years ago. Others are the **descendants** of the hundreds of thousands of people who came from Spain between the mid-1800s and mid-1900s.

Italy's descendants

Most Argentines who are not of Spanish background are descendants of Italians. They came between the mid-1800s and mid-1900s, escaping a life of poverty and **oppression** in their **homeland**. Today, it is not unusual to hear Italian spoken on the streets of some city neighborhoods. Italian culture has influenced Argentina's food, clothing, and entertainment. Even the Spanish spoken by most Argentines is filled with Italian words, accents, and pronunciations.

This vendor proudly shows off a gramophone at an outdoor market in Buenos Aires.

A young girl stands on the balcony of her family's apartment, looking out at the street below.

Other European ancestors

The descendants of many other European peoples live throughout Argentina. Immigrants came from the British Isles, France, Russia, Germany, Austria, Switzerland, and Poland, seeking a better life. Most settled in cities, especially in Buenos Aires, where they lived in neighborhoods with others from their homeland. These neighborhoods still exist today. Many villages in the countryside also have European roots, which are celebrated with traditional festivals, foods, clothing, music, and dance.

Native Americans in Argentina

Today, Argentina's Native peoples make up a very small part of the country's population. Of the 50,000 Native Argentines in the country, the largest group is the Mapuche, also called the Araucano. They live in remote areas of the Andes and Patagonia. Other groups include the Guaraní and Diaguita peoples of the far northwest. Most Native Argentines live in small communities and work as farmers or craftspeople, selling their work to tourists.

Centuries ago, hundreds of thousands of Native peoples lived in Argentina. European settlers and soldiers killed many and drove others from the land. Still other Native peoples died from the diseases that the Europeans brought from their homelands. Although Native peoples who married Europeans have many living descendants today, most of their beliefs and traditions have faded into history.

13

Buenos Aires

Buenos Aires is one of the world's great cities. It is both Argentina's capital and its largest city, with a population of about eleven million. Each day in downtown Buenos Aires, the wide, tree-lined avenues bustle with traffic as millions of people go to work in modern office towers and factories. To relax, they sit and talk in the city's squares and parks, browse at newsstands, eat in cafés, window-shop, or go to a movie.

A taste of Europe

Buenos Aires was once a small city, but as millions of immigrants flooded into Argentina from Europe, it grew into a huge, wealthy city. It was replanned and expanded by **architects** who modeled it after European cities, especially Paris. Today, the streets of Buenos Aires look much like those in Europe's large cities. Old and new shops, restaurants, and apartment buildings stand side by side with galleries and museums.

What's in a name?

In 1536, a group of Spaniards settled at the site of Buenos Aires. They gave their settlement a very long name: *Cuidad de Nuestra Señora Santa María de los Buenos Aires,* or the "City of Our Lady Saint Mary of the Fair Winds." They chose this name to honor the **saint** to whom sailors prayed for good winds. Within a few years, the Spaniards were driven from the area by local Native peoples. After several more attempts to build settlements in this area, the Spaniard Juan de Garay finally succeeded in 1580. In time, the city became known simply as Buenos Aires.

People rush home from school and work on the busy **calle** *Florida.*

"People of the port"

People who live in Buenos Aires are called *porteños,* or "people of the port," because their city has long been the country's major seaport. *Porteños* come from many different backgrounds. Some are new immigrants. Others are the descendants of immigrants who settled in Buenos Aires many years ago. Still others are people who moved from the countryside in search of better jobs, education, and health care.

Plaza de Mayo

At the center of Buenos Aires is Plaza de Mayo. Plaza de Mayo means "May Square." The name honors the month in 1810 when the country began its war of independence against Spain. Plaza de Mayo is a large open area, with palm trees and flower gardens. It is surrounded by some of the country's most important government buildings. The old town hall, called the Cabildo, and the Casa Rosada, the grand, pink-colored offices of Argentina's president, stand across from each other, divided by the Plaza.

(above) Factories and tall buildings stretch out from the port on the Río de la Plata, or "Silver River," in Buenos Aires.

*(top) In the middle of Plaza de Mayo, an obelisk, or tall, four-sided pillar, reminds people of May 25, 1810, the day **porteños** gathered at the Cabildo and decided to fight for their freedom.*

15

The center of it all

Many Argentines consider Plaza de Mayo to be the center of the entire country because so many important national events take place there. Thousands of people often pack the square to hear their leaders speak. Important political decisions are made daily in the Casa Rosada. The Plaza is also a place of protest, made famous by the Mothers of Plaza de Mayo. Each Thursday, these mothers gather to demand to know what happened to their missing children, who were kidnapped by Argentina's former military government.

On the streets

Shops, clubs, restaurants, and cafés in Buenos Aires stay open so late that it is common for the sidewalks to be as busy at 1:00 a.m. as they are in the middle of the afternoon. One of the city's most important streets is called 9 de Julio, or "Ninth of July," in honor of Argentina's day of independence. It is the world's widest avenue, measuring 460 feet (140 meters) across. Another busy downtown street is *calle* Florida, which is lined with stores and closed to motor traffic.

The pink color of the Casa Rosada was created by mixing the fat and blood of cattle with the limestone used to make its walls.

La Boca is a barrio, or neighborhood, in Buenos Aires that is famous for its brightly colored houses.

Though Argentina's other cities are not as large as Buenos Aires, each one has its own personality, with its own industries, local history, and important landmarks.

Town planning

Many Argentine cities were designed in a Spanish style, with a central plaza, or square, whose four corners point to the north, east, south, and west. An old church and town hall border the plaza. In the center stands a monument to an important event or hero. The city streets extend from the four corners of the plaza. Apartment buildings, food markets, restaurants, and shops stand along these streets. Sidewalk cafés are on practically every corner. Streets have similar names from town to town. They are named after other countries, important historic dates, and Argentine heroes.

(right) A tower rises from the rooftop of the University of Córdoba. The university was founded in 1613, making it the oldest university in Argentina.

(below) San Carlos de Bariloche sits at the edge of Lake Nahuel Huapi.

Historic Córdoba

Located between the Andes and the Pampa plains, Córdoba is Argentina's second-largest city. It was founded in 1573, and is one of the country's oldest Spanish settlements. Córdoba's age is reflected in its many old buildings, some dating from the period of Spanish rule. The city also boasts the country's oldest university, which dates back almost 400 years. Today, Córdoba is a lively agricultural center, where crops and livestock are sold.

Industrial Rosario

Rosario, in eastern Argentina, is the country's third-largest city. Most of the factories in this industrial center process food, such as meat, sugar, and wheat. Rosario sits on the Paraná River. It was founded in 1725, but did not start to grow until 1850 when it became one of Argentina's major ports. Today, farmers and manufacturers **export** large amounts of meat and grain from Rosario to countries around the world.

School children take turns sledding down a snowy hill in Ushuaia.

San Carlos de Bariloche

San Carlos de Bariloche, a town whose name is often shortened to Bariloche, is a popular tourist resort in the southern Andes. Visitors say the town reminds them of towns in Switzerland. Like Swiss towns, Bariloche is surrounded by snowcapped mountains, green meadows, and clear, cold lakes. Swiss immigrants founded the town in 1905 and built many of its chalet-style buildings. Among other attractions, tourists enjoy Bariloche's winter festival and its famous chocolate.

Ushuaia

Ushuaia, on the distant island of Tierra del Fuego, is farther south than any other city in the world. In recent years, the Argentine government has encouraged people to move to Ushuaia and work in its growing industries, especially assembling electronic equipment. Ushuaia has also become a popular tourist town. From its port, travelers during the summer months take cruises to the icy shores of Antarctica, about 600 miles (965 kilometers) away.

Neon signs crowd the main street in Salta.

Mendoza in the mountains

Mendoza is known throughout Argentina as the country's center of winemaking. The city sits on the dry slopes of the Andes, where conditions are ideal for growing vast **vineyards**. Mendoza has many open spaces and few tall buildings. Since it was destroyed by an earthquake in 1861, its buildings have been built low to the ground to better withstand tremors.

Salta

The historic city of Salta, founded in 1582, lies in Argentina's northwest. It has many old buildings from the years of Spanish rule, when the city was a trading center. Today, Salta's main industries are based on farming and mining. Its festivals and other cultural events attract many tourists.

Crops and livestock

Argentina is a world leader in farming. Its main products are cattle and grains such as wheat and corn. These farm products are essential to Argentina's food processing and leather industries, and to people and businesses all over the world.

Rich farmlands

Argentina's countryside is dotted with homes, villages, and small towns, all of which are supported by farming. Argentina has some of the best land in the world for growing crops. The black topsoil, or top layer of earth, of the Pampa plains is especially rich in the **nutrients** that wheat, corn, and alfalfa need to grow. Ideal pastureland for sheep and cattle is found throughout the country, especially in the Pampas, Mesopotamia, and northern Patagonia.

Seeds, fruits, and sweets

Besides grains, Argentina grows many other crops. Linseed, flaxseed, and sunflowers grow in the eastern Pampas. The natural oils in these crops are removed and then used in cooking. To the north and west of the Pampas, the climate is hotter and well-suited to growing oranges, grapefruits, lemons, bananas, and sugar cane. Grown on large farms called *ingenios,* sugar cane is harvested by hand before it is processed for sugar and **molasses.** On the hot, dry Andes slopes, grape vines grow in thousands of vineyards. These vines are picked by hand between February and April, the Argentine fall season.

(above right) A farmer pours grain into a seed sowing machine on the Pampas.

(right) A farmer inspects his corn crop on the Pampas.

In some parts of Argentina, farmers still use equipment pulled by mules to tend their fields.

Tea country

Argentine farmers in the north grow many varieties of tea leaves that the British introduced over 100 years ago. Although tea is not popular in Argentina, it is exported. The Argentines prefer a bitter drink called *mate*. It is brewed with the dried leaves of an evergreen bush, the *yerba mate,* which grows in northern Argentina. Thousands of farmers in Mesopotamia harvest the *yerba* leaves by hand.

Cattle ranching

Cattle ranching is a huge industry in Argentina. Farmers have raised cattle on the Pampa plains for over 400 years. Countless herds, each made up of thousands of animals, roam ranches. Many cattle are raised for their milk, but most are raised for their beef, a favorite Argentine food. Beef is also a major export, especially world-famous Argentine corned beef.

*A girl inspects **yerba** leaves, which will then be packed in crates and transported to various parts of Argentina.*

Have you any wool?

The drier, wilder areas of Argentina, such as Patagonia, are ideal for raising sheep. Often, the sheep are tended by shepherds who live in homes in isolated areas. Most of the tens of millions of sheep are raised for wool, which is sold to **textile** factories in Argentina and overseas. The most common breed of wool sheep is the Merino, which has a thick coat that protects the sheep from cold, blustery winds.

On the range

In Argentina, most cattle and sheep are raised on enormous ranches called *estancias*. An *estancia's* large herds are left out to graze on the open range year-round. Ranchers do not have to provide food or shelter for their animals because of the plentiful grass and moderate temperatures on the plains.

There are many jobs to be done at *estancias*. The wealthy landowners who own the ranches hire managers and farmhands to do the daily work. In return, the workers are paid a small salary and are given a place to live. Many tenant farmers, called *colonos*, and their families also live on *estancias*. Landowners give them a house and a plot of land to grow crops. The landowners then sell the crops and give a percentage of the money from the sale to the *colonos*. A large *estancia* can have as many as 20 *colonos* on its land.

The heart of the *estancia*

The owners, farmhands, and *colonos* of an *estancia* live at the heart of the ranch, in buildings that look like a small village. Both the *estancia's* owner and manager live in a big, main house. Surrounding this house are separate, smaller quarters for the farmhands. *Colonos* and their families live further from the main house. Corrals often sit empty, waiting for the season when the livestock will be herded in from the fields for branding, shearing, or shipping to market. Some *estancias* also have a bakery, vegetable garden, small supply store, library, and school.

(top) Wealthy owners of estancias *live in huge homes with their families.*

The *gauchos*

Gauchos are cowboys who herd livestock and do farm chores on *estancias*. They have their own quarters at the center of the ranch, but often sleep under the stars while they are herding thousands of cattle or sheep on the range. Many Argentines admire the *gauchos'* rugged lifestyle. *Gauchos* often spend all day on horseback, skillfully rounding up animals with the help of their dogs. If they are not herding, they spend their time caring for their horses or mending the *estancia's* fences, gates, and equipment.

Round up!

Estancias get very busy when the season comes to round up the livestock. On a beef farm, *gauchos* round up cattle once a year so that they can be weighed. The cattle are then shipped live, by truck, to markets in Buenos Aires, Rosario, and La Plata, where they are sold.

On a sheep ranch, *gauchos* round up the animals so that they can be sheared by work crews called *esquiladores. Esquiladores* travel from ranch to ranch during the springtime. Crew members take pride in their quick work. The fastest workers claim they can shear an entire sheep in under a minute!

Gauchos *round up a herd of cattle to be transported to the markets in Buenos Aires.*

Esquiladores *race to see who can shear a sheep the fastest.*

Much of Argentina has a large, modern transportation network. Buenos Aires is the country's center. It is linked to every major town or city by roads, railroads, or air routes. In places that do not have modern transportation, such as remote parts of the countryside, it is common to see people using horses and sometimes buggies to get around.

Taking the train

Argentina's railroad system is used mainly to transport goods, but people also take the train when traveling long distances or for scenic trips. One of the most famous railway routes in the country is located in Salta. It is nicknamed *el tren de las nubes,* or "the railway to the clouds," because it climbs through spectacular mountain scenery in the Andes. Trains must travel through 21 mountain tunnels, cross more than 40 tall bridges, and zigzag and make 360-degree loops to climb the steepest slopes.

La Trochita, in Patagonia, is a railway line famous for the odd things that happen along its route. The old steam trains used on La Trochita have been forced off the tracks many times by ice, wind, and even collisions with cows!

Boys ride horseback on a country road in Patagonia.

"The railway to the clouds" runs 136 miles (219 kilometers) through tunnels and over bridges in Salta in northwestern Argentina.

Taxis crowd a busy street in downtown Buenos Aires.

Riding the roads

Driving in Argentina is not easy. Roads can be full of potholes and many are poorly paved or are just made of gravel. Rains turn country roads into mud. In the mountains, landslides and avalanches block the way. Bulldozers are often used to plow through the mud, snow, and rubble.

Crowded *colectivos*

Buses called *colectivos* carry local residents back and forth to work. When you hop onto a crowded *colectivo*, prepare for a wild ride! Drivers are known for racing their rattling buses through the streets at breakneck speeds. When the *colectivo* lurches to a stop, the doors pop open and passengers push their way to the back to get off while new passengers leap on in the front. Then, without much warning, the driver slams the doors shut and the bus zooms off to its next stop.

By the roadside

While traveling on Argentina's roads, it is not uncommon to come upon roadside shrines. Shrines are small places dedicated to saints or heroes where people pray and leave candles, money, or other **offerings**. They believe that these offerings will bring them good fortune. Many shrines in Argentina honor La Difunta Correa, a woman who is said to have died of thirst in the desert during the 1840s. Her baby, who she was carrying, miraculously survived. Today, motorists often stop at shrines dedicated to La Difunta Correa and leave her a bottle of water as an offering to quench her thirst.

Industry and resources

Most of Argentina's industries are based on agriculture. Food processing, as well as leather and textile manufacturing, all depend on the country's plentiful crops and large livestock herds. In the last 50 years, however, Argentina has developed new industries, including some based on the county's natural resources. Many people now work to produce oil, steel, cement, chemicals, and automobiles. Millions more, especially in Buenos Aires, work in banking and health care, or work for the government.

Many minerals

Mining is a major industry in Argentina. Mines are located mainly in the Andes, sometimes high in the mountains. Salt, sulfur, coal, iron, zinc, and lead are the most common minerals. **Surveyors** have also found deeply buried deposits of the metal for which Argentina was named — silver.

Logs and lumber

Most logging is done in the Gran Chaco, where huge areas of local forests have been cleared for lumber. The trees of the Gran Chaco are prized for their hard, durable wood. The quebracho tree has particularly hard wood. Its name means "ax breaker." The quebracho is also a source of tannin, an important chemical used to make leather.

(left) A salt mine worker, with pick in hand, prepares to dig at the Salinas Grandes, or "Great Salt Mines," in northwest Argentina.

(below) A freighter, loaded with logs, is ready to leave the port of San Isidro near Buenos Aires.

The energy industry

Argentina has a very large energy industry. Its major oil fields in Patagonia pump out millions of barrels of oil each year. This amount meets nearly all of the country's fuel needs. Natural gas, which is used for heating homes, also comes from this region.

Hydroelectric generators, which use churning water to create electric power, have been built in many places to supply homes and offices with electricity. The Yacyretá *Apipe*, a generating station shared with Argentina's neighbors Brazil and Paraguay, changes the force of Iguazú Falls into electric energy. A few **nuclear power** plants also produce electricity from locally mined **uranium.**

A troubled economy

For most of the last century, Argentina was a troubled land. Military leaders took over the government many times. This instability made business people reluctant to invest in Argentine companies because they feared they would lose their money. Without this money, it was hard for modern industries to grow. Today, Argentina has a stable **democratic** government and one of the fastest-growing economies in South America. Many companies from Europe and the United States have opened offices and factories there.

Grain from across the country is shipped to factories in Buenos Aires, where it is made into flour and other products.

Workers repair a train engine on the Metropolitano railway.

27

Plants and wildlife

*The ombú is a symbol in **gaucho** culture. The giant herb, which grows on the Pampas, once provided the gauchos with shade and shelter.*

Many species of wildlife live throughout Argentina. Each of the country's regions, from desert to jungle, has its own kinds of plants and animals. Many species are unique to South America. Others, such as cattle, horses, and certain plants, were brought from overseas.

Tremendous trees

Many of the tree species found throughout Argentina today were brought by settlers in the last 500 years. These include gingkoes from China and Japan, oaks from England, and blue-blossomed chinaberry or paradise trees from the Middle East.

The ombú looks like a tree, but it is actually a giant herb. Its wood is so soft that it can be cut with a knife. Ombús cannot be used for construction or firewood, but they provide lots of shade.

Dinosaur bones

Millions of years ago, Argentina was home to many dinosaurs. Today, the country has some of the world's most important fossil sites. One well-known site is the Valle de la Luna, or Moon Valley, where over 60 species of fossilized animals have been found.

Argentina's most incredible dinosaurs include the ancient *Herrerasaurus*, which lived 230 million years ago. The *Gigantosaurus carolinii* was a meat-eater even more gigantic than the *Tyranosaurus Rex*. The *Argentinosaurus huiculensis*, named in part after Argentina, is one of the largest plant-eaters ever discovered.

In the bush

Neñeos are round thornbushes that have adapted to life in the dry parts of Argentina. They grow close to the ground, to protect themselves from harsh winds, and are anchored to the earth by a taproot. This root is very long so that neñeos, which receive little rainwater, can draw moisture from deep underground. Seeds from other plants, which would die if exposed to the harsh weather, often thrive when protected inside a neñeo bush. For this reason, people sometimes plant young trees in a neñeo. While protected by the bush, the tree establishes its roots and grows strong. Eventually, however, the tree sucks away the neñeo's water and nutrients, killing it.

The male Andean condor has a caruncle, or fleshy growth, on its head. It uses the caruncle to intimidate its enemies.

Thorny neñeo bushes grow in the Andes mountains, where they protect other plants and trees from harsh weather conditions.

The Andean condor

Argentina is home to many kinds of birds, from tropical toucans to Antarctic penguins. Among the most spectacular is the world's largest bird of prey, the Andean condor. It makes its home in the high cliffs of the Andes mountains. This condor's wingspan is an amazing twelve feet (3.6 meters) wide! Andean condors breed only once every two years, and female birds lay just two eggs. After they hatch, the chicks need constant care for an entire year, until they learn to fly. Today, this giant bird is endangered, or threatened with extinction, because of hunting and the destruction of its **habitat**.

Other interesting birds

Many different birds make the Pampa plains their home. The ñandu, which looks like an ostrich, is one of the more unusual species. It was once a favorite food of Native Argentines and *gauchos*, but today few are left and they are protected from hunters. Ñandus, which stand about 5 feet (1.5 meters) tall, do not fly. Instead, they run across the countryside on their long, powerful legs. Another unusual bird, the hornero, makes its nest on top of fences and electrical posts. These nests look like the old-fashioned, beehive-shaped ovens that Argentines once used. As a result, horneros, which is Spanish for "beehive ovens," are commonly called "oven birds."

The armored armadillo

The name "armadillo" is Spanish for "little armored one." This animal's name comes from the bony, armor-like plates that protect its body. When it is in danger, an armadillo will scrunch itself into a tight ball that its enemies cannot pierce. Armadillos live mainly on the Pampa plains. They are nocturnal, or active at night, which is the best time to hunt their prey of small animals and insects.

The camel family

Several members of the camel family live in Argentina, especially in the high Andes. These include the guanaco, vicuña, alpaca, and llama. They do not have humps like their camel cousins overseas, but like camels they are able to survive in very dry regions. The wild guanaco and vicuña are valued for their fine coats. The other two species are domesticated, or tame. People raise the alpaca for its wool and the llama to work as a **pack animal**.

(left) A guanaco looks for plants and grass to eat in the Valdés Peninsula.

(below) The hairy armadillo grows white or brown hair on its legs and belly and thick bristles between the plates on its back.

(above) Elephant seals and sea lions are a common sight on the shore of the Valdés Peninsula.

(above) The South American coral snake is often called the "false coral snake." Unlike its North American cousin, the venom of the South American coral snake is harmless to human beings.

(left) Magellanic penguins feed each other squid and small fish from the waters surrounding the Valdés Peninsula.

The elephant seal

Each year, thousands of elephant seals make their home on Argentina's Atlantic coast. These seals are named for the male's long, dangling nose. The female seals are much smaller than the enormous males, who can reach an astounding 21 feet (6.5 meters) in length and can weigh over 7700 pounds (3500 kilograms). The male seals frequently battle to control the beaches where the female seals live. Their fights are spectacular and often very bloody.

The Valdés Peninsula

The Valdés Peninsula is one of Argentina's most famous **nature reserves**. Located on the Atlantic coast, the peninsula attracts hundreds of bird species, including Magellanic penguins. These swimming birds build their nests, lay eggs, and raise their chicks on the peninsula's far southern shores. Valdés is also the breeding ground for sea lions, elephant seals, and southern right whales. The peninsula's land animals include ñandus, guanacos, and foxes.

Glossary

ancestor A person from whom one is descended

archtitect A person who designs buildings

canyon A narrow, deep opening in the earth, formed by the flow of water

capital A city where the government of a state or country is located

culture The customs, beliefs, and arts of a distinct group of people

democratic Elected by the people

descendant A person who can trace his or her family roots to a certain family or group

export To sell goods to another country

fertile Able to produce abundant crops or vegetation

glacier A very large, slow-moving chunk of ice

habitat The area or environment in which plants or animals are normally found

homeland An area that is identified with a particular group of people

immigrant A person who settles in another country

livestock Farm animals

mineral A naturally occurring, non-living substance obtained through mining

molasses A dark, thick syrup made from raw sugar

nature reserve A park where wildlife is protected from hunters and is observed by scientists and tourists

nuclear power Energy that is created when atoms come together or split apart

nutrient A substance that a living thing needs in order to grow

offering A gift presented to a god as a sign of worship

oppression Cruel or unfair treatment by a more powerful person or group, usually a government

pack animal An animal that is used to carry large loads

rain shadow A dry area where air has lost its moisture, usually a mountain

saint A person through whom God has performed miracles, according to the Christian church

surveyor A person who measures the boundaries and heights of land

textile A fabric or cloth

tropical Hot and humid

uranium A heavy, toxic, radioactive material that is used for nuclear power and to make nuclear weapons

vineyard An orchard where grapes are grown

Index

1 2 3 4 5 6 7 8 9 0 Printed in the USA 5 4 3 2 1 0 9 8 7 6